Falconry for Kids
Certería Para Niños
by Georgette Baker

Published by Cantemos bilingual books and music San Diego, CA
Email jarjetb@writeme.com

Translation by Georgette Baker

Falconry for Kids

Certería Para Niños

By Georgette Baker

What is falconry? Falconry is hunting, with a trained bird of prey: a falcon, a hawk, an

eagle or a vulture. In falconry, a wild animal in its natural environment, like a rabbit, is

Being hunted with the help of a trained bird of prey.

¿Que es la cetrería? La cetrería es la caza, con un ave de presa adiestrado: un halcón, un águila

O un buitre. En la cetrería, un animal salvaje en su hábito natural, como un conejo, está siendo

perseguido con la ayuda de un ave de presa adiestrado.

There are two traditional terms used to describe a person involved in falconry: a falconer flies a falcon; an austringer flies a hawk, some vultures or an eagle. In modern falconry, the Harris Hawk are often used.

Hay dos términos tradicionales usados para describir a una persona involucrada en la cetrería: un halconero es el cuidador del ave, un cetrero vuela un halcón, un "austringer"(en inglés) vuela un halcón, algunos buitres o águilas. En la cetrería moderna se utiliza a menudo el Halcón Harris.

Falconry can be traced back to ancient times. Long before people started writing things down. It was practiced in many parts of the world. We know this from ancient paintings, drawings, carvings and sculptures.

La cetrería se remonta a la antigüedad, mucho antes que la escritura. Fué practicado en muchas partes del mundo. Lo sabemos por antiguos dibujos, pinturas, obras talladas y esculturas.

It was practiced by Mongolian soldiers to supplement food sources, it was a symbol of status in China and was popular in Medieval Europe as an important part of a gentleman's education, a sport for kings and the common man. Shakespeare may have practice falconry.

Los soldados mongoles lo practicaban para completar sus fuentes de alimentos, era un símbolo de suceso en la China y fue muy popular en Europa medieval como parte importante de la educación de un caballero, disfrutaban tanto los reyes como los hombres comunes. Es posible que Shakespeare practicaba la cetrería.

Today people of all ages can learn, from professional falconers, how to handle a bird of prey.

Hoy en día personas de todas las edades, con la ayuda de cetreros profesionales, pueden

prender cómo manejar un ave de presa.

This is a talon. A talon is the claw of a bird of prey, its primary hunting tool. The talons are very important; without them, most birds of prey would not be able to catch their food.

Esta es una garra.

Las garras de un ave de presa, son su herramienta de caza principal. Las garras son muy importantes; Sin ellas, la mayoría de las aves de presa no serían capases de atrapar su comida.

The talons of birds of prey would tear into the flesh of the falconer if he did not use a heavy form of protection like the gauntlet. Gauntlets are gloves made from leather which cover the hand , wrist and arm of the falconer from the extremely sharp talons.

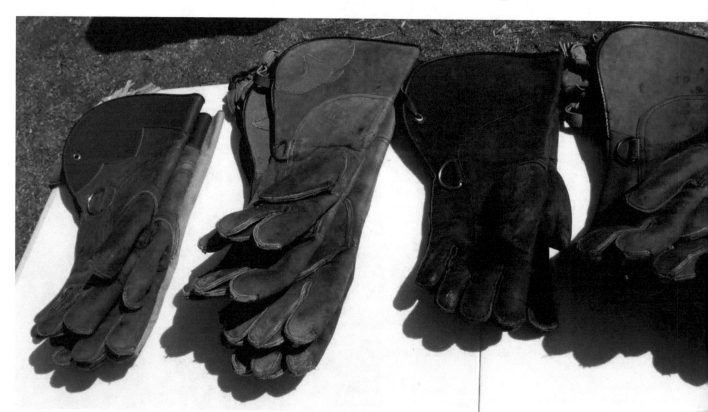

Las garras de las aves de rapiña pueden lastimar al cetrero si él no utiliza una forma de protección, como el guantelete. Guanteletes son guantes hechos de cuero que cubren la mano, la muñeca y el brazo del cetrero y lo protege de las garras muy afiladas.

Without the gauntlet, the talons of the raptor would cut into the flesh of the arm.

Sin el guantelete las garras del raptor cortarían al brazo.

This is a Harris Hawk.

Este es un halcón Harris.

Possibly, the best rabbit or hare raptor available anywhere, the Harris Hawk is also skilled at catching birds. Often raised in captivity, the Harris Hawk is popular because of its temperament and abilities. The Harris Hawk is found in the wild living and hunting in groups or packs like wolves do. This social behavior is not observed in any other bird of prey species .

Posiblemente, el mejor cazador de conejo o liebre disponible en cualquier lugar, el halcón Harris, también es adepto en la captura de aves.

A menudo criados en cautividad, el halcón Harris es muy popular debido a su temperamento y habilidades. El halcón de Harris silvestre se encuentra

viviendo en grupos y suele cazar en cooperación similar a los del lobo. Son muy sociales, un comportamiento que no se observa en otras aves de presa.

This Harris Hawk appears large but only weighs about 2 pounds! The skeletal bones are light and their muscles very strong.

¡Este halcón Haris aparenta ser grande pero pesa menos de dos libras! Los huesos de su esqueleto son livianos y sus músculos muy fuertes.

Here is some basic falconry information.

Stand straight, left arm extended, with gauntlet on. Right arm must be down and held close to the body and back should be turned to arriving bird.

Aquí está un poco de información básica.sobre la cetrería

Párese derecho, el brazo izquierdo extendido, con el guantelete puesto. El brazo derecho debe estar abajo y cerca del cuerpo. Y la espalda debe de estar volteada hacia el ave que llega.

Allow the bird to land on your gauntlet.

Permita que el pájaro aterrice en su guantelete.

Turn your body, left arm extended supporting bird ,

right arm down and close to body.

Gira el cuerpo, brazo izquierdo extendido soportando

al pájaro, brazo derecho hacia abajo y cerca al

cuerpo.

23

It takes patience and time to train a bird of prey to hunt for you. Taking care of it is not easy. The wild bird is always wild and is never to be pet or cuddled. They stay with their Falconer because they choose to but are always able to leave and not return.

Toma paciencia y tiempo para entrenar a una ave de rapiña que cace por ti. Cuidarlo no es fácil. Un pájaro silvestre siempre será silvestre y no debe de ser acariciado ni abrazado. Ellos permanecen con sus cetreros porque lo eligen pero siempre son capaces de irse y de no regresar.

Many birds of prey are used in falconry. Often falconers catch and train their own birds. Now you know something about this ancient sport!

Se utilizan muchas aves de presa en la cetrería. A menudo cetreros capturan y entrenan sus propias aves. ¡Ahora sabes algo acerca de este deporte antiguo !

Author, Georgette Baker and a bird of prey she rescued in Guayaquil, Ecuador in 1976.

Autora, Georgette Baker y un ave de presa que rescató en Guayaquil, Ecuador en 1976.

CANTEMOS –bilingual books and music 2013-2014

Cuentos y Canciones $12.95

Bilingual CD of songs and stories in Spanish & English including the ABC's, the Little Red Hen, The Story of Ferdinand, My Little Shadow, Days of the Week, El Arroyo, Las Estrellas, Los Abuelitos. Appropriate for all ages. Fun, educational, ESL or Spanish language learners.

Patriotic American Songs

Canciones Patrióticas $10.95

Bilingual Pledge of Allegiance, Yankee Doodle, Star Spangled Banner, Grand Old Flag, America the Beautiful

FUNICS $12.95

Phonics fun songs Traditional songs are transformed to enhance Spanish phonemic awareness. CD and book

Las Fabulas de Esopo/

Aesop's Fables CD $12.95

The Lion and the Mouse
The Crow and the Pitcher
The Fox and the Rooster
La Zorra y el Cuervo
The Sun and the Wind

Multicultural Stories/ Cuentos Multiculturales

Chocolate
The Blind Man and the Elephant
The Origin of the Chinese Zodiac
The Origin of Death Native American tale
The Distant Fire African tale about justice

Bilingual CD $12.95

Settle Down Sounds

10 three minute, simple relaxation exercises for the classroom. All ages $9.95

Canciones Infantiles

Spanish Songs for Kids $15

Las Pollitas/The Little Chickies
Periquito/Little Parakeet
Con Real y Medio/With Half a Nickel
Canción de Cuna/Sleep My Little One
El Sapito/The Frog

Se Casa Benito/Benito Will Marry
Allá en Jalisco/There in Jalisco
Arroz con Leche/I Like Rice Pudding
Tengo Una Muñeca/I Have a Little Dolly
De Colores/Many Colors   Gusanito/Squiggly Worm
LA CUCARACHA/THE CUCARACHA
CINCO MONITOS/FIVE LITTLE MONKEYS
LA MARIPOSA/THE BUTTERFLY
REY HONRADO/GREAT WISE KING
THE VOWELS/LAS VOCALES
UN HUEVITO/THE EGG

VEO VEO
CON LAS MANOS/WITH MY HANDS
CANCION DE CUNA/SLEEP MY BABY/
NO TENGO SUEÑO/I'M NOT SLEEPY
MI TÍO/MY UNCLE   SILENT NIGHT/NOCHE DE PAZ
Gloria/GLORIA CANTAN   CANTEMOS
CONEJITO/LITTLE RABBIT   JINGLE BELLS/

Sonidos Serenos

WE'RE OFF TO...BILINGUAL SERIES $12.95 EACH

AUSTRALIA- GREAT BARRIER REEF

PERU

KENYA

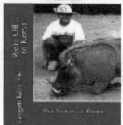

GALAPAGOS

www.simplespanishsongs   Amazon.com   Tel 909-393-8372   email: bakergeorgette@yahoo.com

Purchase orders to Cantemos , 15696 Altamira Dr. Chino Hills, CA 91709

Simple Spanish Songs Songbook

42 songs with piano music use with the following CD's:

Cuentos y Canciones. Cantemos Chiquitos 1 & 2 **$10**

ANDI AND THE GOLD MINE   ANDI Y LA MINA DE
ORO

Adventure in the gold mines of Randsburg, CA with 10 year old

Grandma's Memoirs United by arranged marriage to Abdul by grandparents who had arrived in British Guiana as indentured servants from India. Batoon writes what it was like growing up as a Guianese Indian woman. **$7.95**

NEW!

PERIQUITO Bilingual tale of a little parakeet that goes into the jungle to find his father. **$9.95**

**ALUMINUM CASTLES
CASTILLOS DE ALUMINIO**

WWII from a gunner's view **$12.95**

The autobiography of Maria Karayianni. born and raised in Greece. living with poverty. German occupation and struggling to survive. Told in her own words and translated from her incomplete Greek diary. **$7.95**

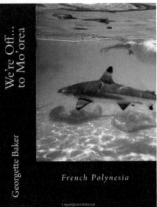

NEW!
We're Off…To Mo'orea
$12.95

NEW! $12.95

www.amazon.com

CPSIA information can be obtained
at www.ICGtesting.com
Printed in the USA
BVHW021546180122
626524BV00002B/5

9781892306609